To Judith, Ann, Fitzwillee,
Wally, Lila Rose, and Izzy, with love.
—T.R.

The editors would like to thank
BARBARA KIEFER, Ph.D.,
Charlotte S. Huck Professor of Children's Literature,
The Ohio State University, and
JACQUE SCHULTZ,
Director, National Shelter Outreach/Companion Animal Programs Advisor,
American Society for the Prevention of Cruelty to Animals,
for their assistance in the preparation of this book.

www.seussville.com

Library of Congress Cataloging-in-Publication Data
Rabe, Tish. Oh, the pets you can get! : all about our animal friends / by Tish Rabe ;
illustrated by Aristides Ruiz and Joe Mathieu. — 1st ed.
    p.   cm. — (The Cat in the Hat's learning library)
ISBN 0-375-82278-X (trade) — ISBN 0-375-92278-4 (lib. bdg.)
1. Pets—Juvenile literature. [1. Pets.]
I. Ruiz, Aristides, ill. II. Mathieu, Joe, ill. III. Title. IV. Series.
SF416.2 .R29 2005
636.088'7—dc22
2003027157

Oh, the Pets You Can Get!

by Tish Rabe

illustrated by Aristides Ruiz and Joe Mathieu

The Cat in the Hat's Learning Library™

Random House 🏠 New York

I'm the Cat in the Hat.

I love pets as you see.

You can meet lots of pets

if you travel with me.

We are off to the faraway
land of Gerpletz,
where they know quite a lot
about caring for pets.

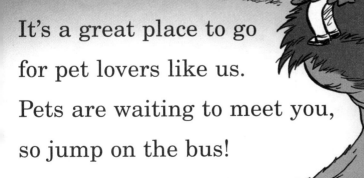

It's a great place to go
for pet lovers like us.
Pets are waiting to meet you,
so jump on the bus!

The first place in Gerpletz
we will visit today
is the Play with Your Pet Park,
where pets come to play.

Dogs and puppies need exercise.
They love to run!
They chase balls and catch toys,
make new friends and have fun.

8

Kittens tumble in heaps
and bat toys with their paws.
Cats climb up on posts and
hold tight with their claws.

In Gerpletz they don't let
any pets play with string.
Pets can get tangled.
That's not a good thing!

Guinea pigs need to get
lots of exercise, too.
There are ramps to be climbed
and tubes to run through.

Rabbits hop all around
and love to explore.
They play "soccer" by pushing
small balls on the floor.

Birds go flying! Their cages
are left open wide.
When they're tired of flying,
they go back inside.

When the pets finish playing,
they run down the street
to the Finer Pet Diner
for something to eat.

There's a lot on the menu,
so each pet can find
the food that for them
is the very best kind.

Mr. Finer serves rabbits
a very fine lunch
of veggies, fruit, hay, and
some pellets to munch.

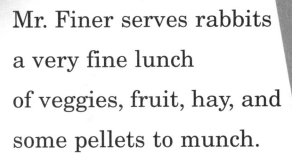

Guinea pigs nibble veggies,
fruit, grass, grain, and seeds.

Clean water is something
that every pet needs.

Mrs. Finer makes cat food
that cats love to eat.
She knows cats and kittens
always like to eat meat.

Our dog Scrunchy likes dog food,
so here's what we do—
feed him dry food or wet food
or mix up the two.

DRY
DOG
FOOD

Birds feed on pellets
and fruit twice a day.
It is served up to them
on a small plastic tray.

Pets want to make friends,
like you and like me!
They want to be part
of your whole family.

CATNIP

With a cat or a dog
you may find—it is true—
that the friend they want most
to spend time with is you!

Some pets get lonely
and think it's more fun
to live with a friend.
So we got more than one.

Every pet that you get
needs a nice place to rest.
The Pet Beds and More store
has only the best.

Here's a beautiful birdcage.
The best cage to buy
is one that has room
so your pet bird can fly.

A dog might like sleeping
on this cozy bed.

Cats might like boxes
or baskets instead.

Guinea pigs like a cage,
but they're glad it is not
sitting right in the sunlight.
They don't like to get hot.

This cage for our rabbit
is known as a hutch.
It takes time to clean it,
but not very much.

Now, my friends in Gerpletz
have just asked me to go
be the host of the
Pets of Gerpletz TV show!

My first guest is a kitten.
I gave him a hat.
In one year this kitten
will turn into a cat.

If you pet your cat gently
and rub her soft fur,
in a minute you might
hear your cat start to purr.

20

When you carry your kitten
(we thought this was neat!),
put one hand around him,
one under his feet.

PETS
OF
GERPLETZ

Rabbits are cute with their long, fuzzy ears. Some rabbits will live from eight to twelve years.

Meet my pet rabbit.
She's known as a Lop.
Her ears don't stand up.
On a Lop, the ears flop.

PETS
of
GERPLETZ

I carry my rabbit
up close to my chest.
That's the way to be carried
that rabbits love best.

Meet these puppies and dogs.
They are glad to meet you!
They are wonderful pets
who are loyal and true.

When I first got my puppy,
I got a surprise.
Some puppies grow up
to be TEN times their size!

You need to train puppies.
When they make mistakes,
understanding and patience
are all that it takes.

If training a puppy
is too hard to do,
older dogs that are trained
might be just right for you.

If your dog ever tries
to give your face a lick,
please don't let him do it.
It could make you sick! (Ick!)

Now the next special guests
I would like you to meet
are these yellow canaries
and sweet parakeets.

Birds are colorful pets.
They can whistle and sing,
and your home will be filled
with the music they bring.

Try this trick with your bird.
It is easy to do it.
Hold your finger straight out—
your bird might fly to it!

We learned this about birds
from our Great-Uncle Mudgie—
a parakeet is also
known as a budgie!

MUDGIE

He taught us about
these canaries we bought.
Male canaries can sing,
but females cannot!

27

Guinea pigs are sweet pets
and they're easy to feed.
If you don't have much space,
they may be what you need.

Guinea pigs like to hide
in the grass or in hay.
They eat all the time—
about six hours a day!

MILD N'
GENTLE
PET
SHAMPOO

Guinea pigs like to get
a warm bath with shampoo.
Dry them in a soft towel,
then brush their fur, too.

Meet Ms. Fuzzy Finwinkle,
the mayor of Gerpletz.
She's an expert on how
to have safe, healthy pets.

Her pets are on leashes
so they cannot stray.
They stay close to her.
They are safer that way.

Her pets all wear tags
with her name and address.
Who do they belong to?
Folks don't have to guess.

When she goes on vacation,
Ms. Finwinkle gets
a pet-sitter or friend who
will care for her pets.

When you care for your pets,
there's a lot you can do
to keep your pets healthy
and YOU healthy, too.

Put detergent up high
so your pets can't get to it.

A houseplant goes where
your pets won't try to chew it.

When cleaning a cage,
wear gloves like we do.
Use hot water and soap.
Wash your hands when you're through.

Keep your toilet lid closed
so your pets do not think
that the water inside it
is for them to drink!

33

There are people with pets,
I am sorry to say,
who for all kinds of reasons
must give them away.

They go to pet shelters.
Right here in Gerpletz
there's a shelter that's full
of all kinds of nice pets.

So if you want a pet,
here is what you can do—
get a pet from a shelter
to take home with you.

DONATIONS

Now, at least once a year
many pets that you get
to stay healthy will need
to go visit a vet.

The vet checks your pet,
listens to his heart beating,
and asks you some questions
like "Is your pet eating?"

A veterinarian,
I'd like to report,
is an animal doctor
called a "vet" for short.

A VET is a
VETERINARIAN

Each time we take one
of our pets to the vet,
we write down what we're told
so that we won't forget.

If your pet doesn't eat,
or does not want to play,
or your pet's losing weight,
see the vet right away!

I know getting a pet
is a big thing to do.
There are questions to answer
and here are a few—

Do you have enough space
for a pet of this size?
Will he have room to play?
Will she get exercise?

Do you have enough time
for your pet every day?
Who will care for your pet
if you must go away?

Now, you may just decide
after meeting these pets
that you are not ready
to get a pet yet.

But if you DO get one,
please don't give it away.
Close to you is the one place
your pet wants to stay.

Take your time to decide
so you know from the start
you can keep it for life

in your home

and your heart.

GLOSSARY

Canary: A small yellow songbird.

Detergent: A chemical substance, either a liquid or a powder, that is used to clean things.

Expert: A person who knows a lot about one special thing.

Hutch: A house for rabbits or other small animals.

Parakeet: A small parrot with a long, pointed tail and bright feathers.

Patience: The ability to react calmly to mistakes or delays.

Shelter: A place where an animal who is lost or doesn't have a home can stay.

Tangled: Knotted together in a twisted mess.

Understanding: The ability to feel and show sympathy.

Veterinarian: A doctor who treats animals.

FOR FURTHER READING

The Berenstain Bears' Trouble with Pets by Stan and Jan Berenstain (Random House, *First Time Books*). Brother and Sister discover the responsibility that comes with a new puppy. For kindergarten and up.

Birds: A Practical Guide to Caring for Your Birds (ASPCA Pet Care Guides for Kids) by Mark Evans (Dorling Kindersley). Find out how to care for your new pet from the experts. For grades 1 and up.

Koko's Kitten by Dr. Francine Patterson, photographs by Ronald H. Cohn (Scholastic). Learn about an unusual but loving relationship between owner and pet in this true story. For grades 1 and up.

The Stray Dog by Marc Simont (HarperCollins). A stray dog adopts a family at a picnic. For kindergarten and up.

Why Do Rabbits Hop? And Other Questions About Rabbits, Guinea Pigs, Hamsters, and Gerbils by Joan Holub, photographs by Anna DiVito (Puffin, *Puffin Easy-to-Read*). All about the small animals that make very popular pets. For kindergarten and up.

INDEX

birds, 11, 26–27
  cage for, 11, 18
  food for, 15
budgies, 27

cages, 11, 18, 19, 33
canaries, 26, 27
cats, 9, 16, 20–21
  bed for, 19
  food for, 14
cleaning, 19, 29, 33

detergent, 32
dogs, 8, 16, 24–25
  bed for, 18
  food for, 14
  training of, 24–25

exercise, 8–11, 38

food, 12–15

guinea pigs, 10, 28–29
  cage for, 19
  food for, 13

health, 32–33, 36–37
houseplants, 33
hutch, 19

kittens, 9, 14, 20–21;
  see also cats

leashes, 30
loneliness, 17

parakeets, 26, 27
pet-sitters, 31, 39
play, 8–11, 38
puppies, 8, 24–25;
  see also dogs

rabbits, 10, 22–23
  cage for, 19
  food for, 13

safety, 9, 19, 30–33
shelters, 34–35
string, 9

tags, 31
toilet, 33
training, 24–25

veterinarians, 36–37

water, 13, 33